Let's Celebrate Latino Holidays

CARNIVAL

Sadie Silva

Enslow
PUBLISHING

Please visit our website, www.enslow.com. For a free color catalog of all our high-quality books, call toll free 1-800-398-2504 or fax 1-877-980-4454.

Library of Congress Cataloging-in-Publication Data
Names: Silva, Sadie, author.
Title: Carnival / Sadie Silva.
Description: New York : Enslow Publishing, [2023] | Series: Let's Celebrate Latino Holidays | Includes index.
Identifiers: LCCN 2021037504 (print) | LCCN 2021037505 (ebook) | ISBN 9781978527164 (library binding) | ISBN 9781978527140 (paperback) | ISBN 9781978527157 (set) | ISBN 9781978527171 (ebook)
Subjects: LCSH: Carnival--Latin America--History--Juvenile literature. | Carnival--Juvenile literature.
Classification: LCC GT4213.5 .S55 2023 (print) | LCC GT4213.5 (ebook) | DDC 394.25098--dc23
LC record available at https://lccn.loc.gov/2021037504LC ebook record available at https://lccn.loc.gov/2021037505

First Edition

Portions of this work were originally authored by Marisa Orgullo and published as *Celebrating Carnival!*. All new material this edition authored by Sadie Silva.

Published in 2023 by
Enslow Publishing
29 E. 21st Street
New York, NY 10010

Copyright © 2023 Enslow Publishing

Designer: Katelyn Reynolds
Interior Layout: Rachel Rising
Editor: Caitie McAneney

Photo credits: Cover, Orchid photho/Shutterstock.com; Cover, pp. 1-4, 6, 8, 10, 12, 14, 16, 18, 20, 22-24 (background) Cienpies Design/Shutterstock.com; Cover, pp. 1, 3, 23, 24 (text box) scoutori/Shutterstock.com; Cover, pp. 1, 3, 23, 24 (text) Cienpies Design/Shutterstock.com; p. 5 BW Press/Shutterstock.com; p. 7 Ron Zmiri/Shutterstock.com; p. 9 Shawn Eastman Photography/Shutterstock.com; p. 11 Celso Pupo/Shutterstock.com; p. 13 Peter Molnar/Shutterstock.com; p. 15 gary yims/Shutterstock.com; p. 17 John de la Bastide/Shutterstock.com; p. 19 Salim October/Shutterstock.com; p. 21 Suzanne C. Grim/Shutterstock.com; p. 22 Lisa Kolbasa/Shutterstock.com.

All rights reserved. No part of this book may be reproduced in any form without permission in writing from the publisher, except by a reviewer.

Printed in the United States of America

Some of the images in this book illustrate individuals who are models. The depictions do not imply actual situations or events.

CPSIA compliance information: Batch #CSENS23: For further information contact Enslow Publishing, New York, New York, at 1-800-398-2504.

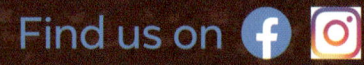

Find us on

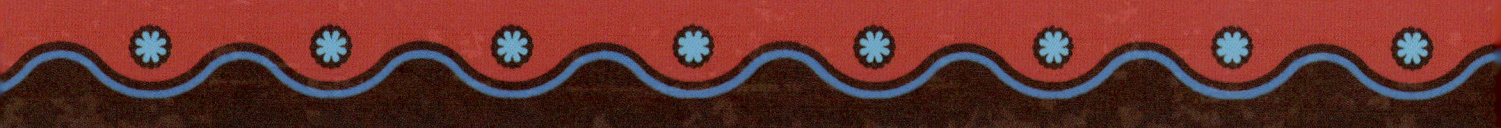

CONTENTS

Celebrate Carnival! 4
Carnival on the Mainland 10
Carnival in the Caribbean 16
Carnival Around the World 20
Glossary 23
For More Information 24
Index 24

Words in the glossary appear in **bold** type the first time they are used in the text.

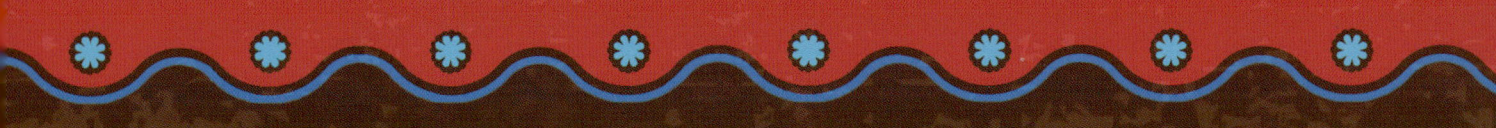

Celebrate Carnival!

Carnival (KAR-nuh-vahl) is a **celebration** of life! It's celebrated all around the world. But the celebrations in Latin America are truly special. Carnival takes place in February or March. People dress up for parades and parties. They wear colorful feathers, masks, makeup, and gems.

Carnival **costumes** have many feathers and gems.

Carnival has a long history with many **roots**. Most famously, it was a time to prepare for Lent. Lent is the 40 days before Easter. During that time, some **Catholics** give up things they enjoy. Carnival helps people have fun before they give up things they like.

People have celebrated Carnival in Latin America for hundreds of years.

Carnival is celebrated differently in different places in Latin America. Each place has its own **traditions** and tastes. They have some things in common though. For example, Carnival often starts on a weekend. It stops the last day before Lent, called Shrove Tuesday.

Many places in Latin America have strong Catholic roots. The Christ the Redeemer statue in Rio de Janeiro, Brazil, is famous.

Carnival on the Mainland

The largest Carnival celebration in the world is in Rio de Janeiro, Brazil. People travel from around the world to celebrate in Rio. Huge parades feature **floats** and **performers**. At night, people go to balls, or dances. They dress up as animals, superheroes, princesses, and devils.

This parade is part of Rio de Janeiro's Carnival celebration.

11

Music and dance are at the heart of Rio's Carnival. Brazilians take part in dance groups called samba schools. Samba is a type of music and dance with European and African roots. During Carnival, samba schools dance in parades alongside colorful floats.

Samba school performers in Carnival parades often wear beautiful costumes.

Carnival is also celebrated in other mainland countries like Argentina, Uruguay, and Mexico. Children make *cascarones* (kas-kah-ROH-nays), or eggshells filled with colorful paper. The children then break them for good luck. Fireworks, live music, and dancing add to the joy of the celebration.

At this Carnival celebration in Mexico, people play music and dance on canal boats.

Carnival in the Caribbean

The islands of the Caribbean also celebrate Carnival. Trinidad and Tobago is a country made up of two islands in the Caribbean. People play and sing a type of music called **calypso** (kuh-LIP-soh), and drummers pound on steel pans. The bands' members wear costumes, and they dance together in the streets.

Steel drum bands provide music for dancers during Carnival in Trinidad.

17

Caribbean Carnival isn't only for adults. Children in Trinidad and Tobago also join in the fun! They dress in big, colorful costumes for a Kiddies Carnival parade. The costumes look like butterflies, flowers, knights on horses, or even jellyfish. They dance to calypso music.

Some kids' costumes are so big they need help to get ready and to walk.

Carnival Around the World

Carnival is celebrated all around the world. In New Orleans, Louisiana, the main part of the celebration is Mardi Gras (MAHR-dee GRAH). Parades with flashy floats crowd the streets. Costumed riders throw strings of colorful beads to visitors. People eat a colorful treat called King Cake.

Mardi Gras, part of Carnival, is the biggest celebration in New Orleans!

21

People celebrate Carnival in Toronto, Canada; London, United Kingdom; Sydney, Australia; and Venice, Italy. The celebration brings joy to people in many countries, especially in Latin America. Each country brings its own music, dances, and costumes to the party!

GLOSSARY

calypso A kind of lively Caribbean music.
Catholic A member of the Roman Catholic church.
celebration A time to show happiness for an event through activities such as eating or playing music.
costume Clothes or masks that make a person look like someone or something else.
float A car or truck used to present art and performances in a parade.
performer A person who performs, or plays music, sings, dances, or acts.
root The cause of something.
tradition Something that has been done for a long time.

FOR MORE INFORMATION

Books

Ponto, Joanna. *Mardi Gras*. New York, NY: Enslow Publishing, 2016.

Williams, Heather DiLorenzo and Marjorie Faulstich Orellana. *Trinidad and Tobago*. New York, NY, Bearport Publishing, 2019.

Websites

Brazil Facts: Discover This Super-Cool Country!
www.natgeokids.com/nz/discover/geography/countries/country-fact-file-brazil/
Learn all about Brazil, including its Carnival, with National Geographic Kids.

Trinidad and Tobago
www.ducksters.com/geography/country.php?country=Trinidad%20and%20Tobago
Explore more fun facts about Trinidad and Tobago.

Publisher's note to educators and parents: Our editors have carefully reviewed these websites to ensure that they are suitable for students. Many websites change frequently, however, and we cannot guarantee that a site's future contents will continue to meet our high standards of quality and educational value. Be advised that students should be closely supervised whenever they access the internet.

INDEX

Brazil, 9, 10, 11, 12
Catholics, 6, 9
calypso, 16, 18
Caribbean, 16, 18
costumes, 5, 13, 16, 18, 19, 20, 22
dance, 10, 12, 14, 15, 16, 17, 18, 22
history, 6

Lent, 6, 8
Mardi Gras, 20, 21
Mexico, 14, 15
parades, 4, 10, 11, 12, 13, 18, 20
samba schools, 12, 13
traditions, 8